PERFUME

ORDER BOOK

Business Name: _Knitting - Notions_

Email:_____

Tel:_____

Mobile:_____

Fax:_____

Order No.	Date Of Order	Name	Total
01	6/3/21	1h 22x white loopy. Set Ready. 8/3.	€25
02	6/3/21	Candy Pink loopy Cardigan only.	€ 15 (little hee.
03	6/3/21	Tonya Murphy - Pink and white	
04	5/3/21.	Orange loopy. Danielle Jurey.	€20

Order No.	Date Of Order	Name	Total
Order No.	Date Of Order	Name	Total

Order No.	Date Of Order	Name	Total

Order No.	Date Of Order	Name	Total
Order No.	Date Of Order	Name	Total

Order No.	Date Of Order	Name	Total

Order No.	Date Of Order	Name	Total
Order No.	Date Of Order	Name	Total

Account Name : _____

Name : _____

Address : _____

_____

Payment Methods

○ Cash on delivery   Amount

○ Check payment   _____

○ Direct bank transfer   Date Paid

○ PayPal   _____

Order Number : _____

Date of order : _____

Ship date : _____

Shipping carrier : _____

Tracking ID : _____

Delivered : _____

Special option

○ Samples sent

○ Gift Message

_____

_____

Product No.	Description	Qty.	Total

Notes:		
	Total	
	Product Cost	
	Postage Cost	
	Tax	
	Profit	

Account Name : _____

Name : _____

Address : _____

_____

Payment Methods

○ Cash on delivery   Amount

○ Check payment   _____

○ Direct bank transfer   Date Paid

○ PayPal   _____

Order Number : _____

Date of order : _____

Ship date : _____

Shipping carrier : _____

Tracking ID : _____

Delivered : _____

Special option

○ Samples sent

○ Gift Message

_____

_____

Product No.	Description	Qty.	Total

Notes:

Total	
Product Cost	
Postage Cost	
Tax	
Profit	

Account details

(🐦) (📷) (f) (👻) (▶) (v) (📌) (in)
○ ○ ○ ○ ○ ○ ○ ○

Account Name : _____

Name : _____

Address : _____

_____

Payment Methods

○ Cash on delivery   Amount

○ Check payment   _____

○ Direct bank transfer   Date Paid

○ PayPal   _____

Order Number : _____

Date of order : _____

Ship date : _____

Shipping carrier : _____

Tracking ID : _____

Delivered : _____

Special option

○ Samples sent

○ Gift Message

_____

_____

Product No.	Description	Qty.	Total

Notes:

Total	
Product Cost	
Postage Cost	
Tax	
Profit	

Account Name : _____

Name : _____

Address : _____

_____

| Payment Methods |

○ Cash on delivery   Amount

○ Check payment   _____

○ Direct bank transfer   Date Paid

○ PayPal   _____

Order Number : _____

Date of order : _____

Ship date : _____

Shipping carrier : _____

Tracking ID : _____

Delivered : _____

| Special option |

○ Samples sent

○ Gift Message

_____

_____

Product No.	Description	Qty.	Total

Notes:		Total	
		Product Cost	
		Postage Cost	
		Tax	
		Profit	

Account Name : _____

Name : _____

Address : _____

_____

Payment Methods

- O Cash on delivery   Amount
- O Check payment   _____
- O Direct bank transfer   Date Paid
- O PayPal   _____

Order Number : _____

Date of order : _____

Ship date : _____

Shipping carrier : _____

Tracking ID : _____

Delivered : _____

Special option

- O Samples sent
- O Gift Message

_____

_____

Product No.	Description	Qty.	Total

Notes:		
	Total	
	Product Cost	
	Postage Cost	
	Tax	
	Profit	

Account Name : _____

Name : _____

Address : _____

_____

Payment Methods

- ○ Cash on delivery   Amount
- ○ Check payment   _____
- ○ Direct bank transfer   Date Paid
- ○ PayPal   _____

Order Number : _____

Date of order : _____

Ship date : _____

Shipping carrier : _____

Tracking ID : _____

Delivered : _____

Special option

- ○ Samples sent
- ○ Gift Message

_____

_____

Product No.	Description	Qty.	Total

Notes:	Total	
	Product Cost	
	Postage Cost	
	Tax	
	Profit	

Left Panel

🐦 📷 f 👻 ▶ v 📌 in
○ ○ ○ ○ ○ ○ ○ ○

Account Name : _____

Name : _____

Address : _____

_____

Payment Methods

- ○ Cash on delivery   Amount
- ○ Check payment   _____
- ○ Direct bank transfer   Date Paid
- ○ PayPal   _____

Right Panel

Order Number : _____

Date of order : _____

Ship date : _____

Shipping carrier : _____

Tracking ID : _____

Delivered : _____

Special option

- ○ Samples sent
- ○ Gift Message

_____

_____

Order Table

Product No.	Description	Qty.	Total

Notes:

Total	
Product Cost	
Postage Cost	
Tax	
Profit	

Account Name : _____

Name : _____

Address : _____

_____

Payment Methods

O Cash on delivery   Amount

O Check payment   _____

O Direct bank transfer   Date Paid

O PayPal   _____

Order Number : _____

Date of order : _____

Ship date : _____

Shipping carrier : _____

Tracking ID : _____

Delivered : _____

Special option

O Samples sent

O Gift Message

_____

_____

Product No.	Description	Qty.	Total

Notes:		Total	
		Product Cost	
		Postage Cost	
		Tax	
		Profit	

Account Name : _____

Name : _____

Address : _____

_____

Order Number : _____

Date of order : _____

Ship date : _____

Shipping carrier : _____

Tracking ID : _____

Delivered : _____

Payment Methods

○ Cash on delivery   Amount

○ Check payment   _____

○ Direct bank transfer   Date Paid

○ PayPal   _____

Special option

○ Samples sent

○ Gift Message

_____

_____

Product No.	Description	Qty.	Total

Notes:		Total	
		Product Cost	
		Postage Cost	
		Tax	
		Profit	

Account Name : _____

Name : _____

Address : _____

_____

Order Number : _____

Date of order : _____

Ship date : _____

Shipping carrier : _____

Tracking ID : _____

Delivered : _____

Payment Methods

○ Cash on delivery   Amount

○ Check payment   _____

○ Direct bank transfer   Date Paid

○ PayPal   _____

Special option

○ Samples sent

○ Gift Message

_____

_____

Product No.	Description	Qty.	Total

Notes:

Total	
Product Cost	
Postage Cost	
Tax	
Profit	

Account Name : _____

Name : _____

Address : _____

_____

Payment Methods

○ Cash on delivery   Amount

○ Check payment   _____

○ Direct bank transfer   Date Paid

○ PayPal   _____

Order Number : _____

Date of order : _____

Ship date : _____

Shipping carrier : _____

Tracking ID : _____

Delivered : _____

Special option

○ Samples sent

○ Gift Message

_____

_____

Product No.	Description	Qty.	Total

Notes:		
	Total	
	Product Cost	
	Postage Cost	
	Tax	
	Profit	

Account Name : _____

Name : _____

Address : _____

_____

Payment Methods

- ○ Cash on delivery
- ○ Check payment
- ○ Direct bank transfer
- ○ PayPal

Amount

_____

Date Paid

_____

Order Number : _____

Date of order : _____

Ship date : _____

Shipping carrier : _____

Tracking ID : _____

Delivered : _____

Special option

- ○ Samples sent
- ○ Gift Message

_____

_____

Product No.	Description	Qty.	Total

Notes:

	Total	
	Product Cost	
	Postage Cost	
	Tax	
	Profit	

Account Name : _____

Name : _____

Address : _____

_____

Payment Methods

- ○ Cash on delivery   Amount
- ○ Check payment   _____
- ○ Direct bank transfer   Date Paid
- ○ PayPal   _____

Order Number : _____

Date of order : _____

Ship date : _____

Shipping carrier : _____

Tracking ID : _____

Delivered : _____

Special option

- ○ Samples sent
- ○ Gift Message

_____

_____

Product No.	Description	Qty.	Total

Notes:		
	Total	
	Product Cost	
	Postage Cost	
	Tax	
	Profit	

Account Name : _____

Name : _____

Address : _____

_____

Payment Methods

O Cash on delivery   Amount

O Check payment   _____

O Direct bank transfer   Date Paid

O PayPal   _____

Order Number : _____

Date of order : _____

Ship date : _____

Shipping carrier : _____

Tracking ID : _____

Delivered : _____

Special option

O Samples sent

O Gift Message

_____

_____

Product No.	Description	Qty.	Total

Notes:		
	Total	
	Product Cost	
	Postage Cost	
	Tax	
	Profit	

Left Panel

(🐦) (📷) (f) (👻) (▶) (v) (P) (in)
○ ○ ○ ○ ○ ○ ○ ○

Account Name : _____

Name : _____

Address : _____

_____

Payment Methods

○ Cash on delivery   Amount

○ Check payment   _____

○ Direct bank transfer   Date Paid

○ PayPal   _____

Right Panel

Order Number : _____

Date of order : _____

Ship date : _____

Shipping carrier : _____

Tracking ID : _____

Delivered : _____

Special option

○ Samples sent

○ Gift Message

_____

_____

Table

Product No.	Description	Qty.	Total

Notes:		Total	
		Product Cost	
		Postage Cost	
		Tax	
		Profit	

Account Name : _____

Name : _____

Address : _____

_____

Payment Methods

○ Cash on delivery   Amount

○ Check payment   _____

○ Direct bank transfer   Date Paid

○ PayPal   _____

Order Number : _____

Date of order : _____

Ship date : _____

Shipping carrier : _____

Tracking ID : _____

Delivered : _____

Special option

○ Samples sent

○ Gift Message

_____

_____

Product No.	Description	Qty.	Total

Notes:		Total	
		Product Cost	
		Postage Cost	
		Tax	
		Profit	

Account Name : _____

Name : _____

Address : _____

_____

Payment Methods

O Cash on delivery   Amount

O Check payment   _____

O Direct bank transfer   Date Paid

O PayPal   _____

Order Number : _____

Date of order : _____

Ship date : _____

Shipping carrier : _____

Tracking ID : _____

Delivered : _____

Special option

O Samples sent

O Gift Message

_____

_____

Product No.	Description	Qty.	Total

Notes:

	Total	
	Product Cost	
	Postage Cost	
	Tax	
	Profit	

Account Name : _____

Name : _____

Address : _____

_____

Order Number : _____

Date of order : _____

Ship date : _____

Shipping carrier : _____

Tracking ID : _____

Delivered : _____

Payment Methods

○ Cash on delivery   Amount

○ Check payment   _____

○ Direct bank transfer   Date Paid

○ PayPal   _____

Special option

○ Samples sent

○ Gift Message

_____

_____

Product No.	Description	Qty.	Total

Notes:	Total	
	Product Cost	
	Postage Cost	
	Tax	
	Profit	

Social Media Icons

Account Name : _____

Name : _____

Address : _____

_____

Payment Methods

- ○ Cash on delivery
- ○ Check payment
- ○ Direct bank transfer
- ○ PayPal

Amount

_____

Date Paid

_____

Order Number : _____

Date of order : _____

Ship date : _____

Shipping carrier : _____

Tracking ID : _____

Delivered : _____

Special option

- ○ Samples sent
- ○ Gift Message

_____

_____

Product No.	Description	Qty.	Total

Notes:

Total	
Product Cost	
Postage Cost	
Tax	
Profit	

Account Name : _____

Name : _____

Address : _____

_____

Order Number : _____

Date of order : _____

Ship date : _____

Shipping carrier : _____

Tracking ID : _____

Delivered : _____

Payment Methods

O Cash on delivery   Amount

O Check payment   _____

O Direct bank transfer   Date Paid

O PayPal   _____

Special option

O Samples sent

O Gift Message

_____

_____

Product No.	Description	Qty.	Total

Notes:

Total	
Product Cost	
Postage Cost	
Tax	
Profit	

Social Media Icons

Account Name : _____

Name : _____

Address : _____

_____

Payment Methods

- ○ Cash on delivery   Amount
- ○ Check payment   _____
- ○ Direct bank transfer   Date Paid
- ○ PayPal   _____

Order Number : _____

Date of order : _____

Ship date : _____

Shipping carrier : _____

Tracking ID : _____

Delivered : _____

Special option

- ○ Samples sent
- ○ Gift Message

_____

_____

Product No.	Description	Qty.	Total

Notes:

Total	
Product Cost	
Postage Cost	
Tax	
Profit	

Account Name : _____

Name : _____

Address : _____

_____

Amount

_____

Date Paid

_____

Order Number : _____

Date of order : _____

Ship date : _____

Shipping carrier : _____

Tracking ID : _____

Delivered : _____

Special option

- O Samples sent
- O Gift Message

_____

_____

Product No.	Description	Qty.	Total

Notes:		
	Total	
	Product Cost	
	Postage Cost	
	Tax	
	Profit	

Account Name : _____

Name : _____

Address : _____

_____

Order Number : _____

Date of order : _____

Ship date : _____

Shipping carrier : _____

Tracking ID : _____

Delivered : _____

Payment Methods

- ○ Cash on delivery   Amount
- ○ Check payment   _____
- ○ Direct bank transfer   Date Paid
- ○ PayPal   _____

Special option

- ○ Samples sent
- ○ Gift Message

_____

_____

Product No.	Description	Qty.	Total

Notes:

Total	
Product Cost	
Postage Cost	
Tax	
Profit	

Account Name : _____

Name : _____

Address : _____

_____

Payment Methods

- O Cash on delivery   Amount
- O Check payment   _____
- O Direct bank transfer   Date Paid
- O PayPal   _____

Order Number : _____

Date of order : _____

Ship date : _____

Shipping carrier : _____

Tracking ID : _____

Delivered : _____

Special option

- O Samples sent
- O Gift Message

_____

_____

Product No.	Description	Qty.	Total

Notes:			
	Total	
	Product Cost	
	Postage Cost	
	Tax	
	Profit	

Account Name : _____

Name : _____

Address : _____

_____

Payment Methods

○ Cash on delivery   Amount

○ Check payment   _____

○ Direct bank transfer   Date Paid

○ PayPal   _____

Order Number : _____

Date of order : _____

Ship date : _____

Shipping carrier : _____

Tracking ID : _____

Delivered : _____

Special option

○ Samples sent

○ Gift Message

_____

_____

Product No.	Description	Qty.	Total

Notes:

	Total	
	Product Cost	
	Postage Cost	
	Tax	
	Profit	

Twitter ◯ Instagram ◯ Facebook ◯ Snapchat ◯ YouTube ◯ Vimeo ◯ Pinterest ◯ LinkedIn ◯

Account Name : _____

Name : _____

Address : _____

_____

Payment Methods

◯ Cash on delivery

◯ Check payment

◯ Direct bank transfer

◯ PayPal

Amount

_____

Date Paid

_____

Order Number : _____

Date of order : _____

Ship date : _____

Shipping carrier : _____

Tracking ID : _____

Delivered : _____

Special option

◯ Samples sent

◯ Gift Message

_____

_____

Product No.	Description	Qty.	Total

Notes:	Total	
	Product Cost	
	Postage Cost	
	Tax	
	Profit	

Account

Account Name : _____

Name : _____

Address : _____

_____

Payment Methods

- O Cash on delivery   Amount
- O Check payment _____
- O Direct bank transfer   Date Paid
- O PayPal _____

Order

Order Number : _____

Date of order : _____

Ship date : _____

Shipping carrier : _____

Tracking ID : _____

Delivered : _____

Special option

- O Samples sent
- O Gift Message

_____

_____

Product No.	Description	Qty.	Total

Notes:		Total	
		Product Cost	
		Postage Cost	
		Tax	
		Profit	

Social Media Icons

Twitter · Instagram · Facebook · Snapchat · YouTube · Vimeo · Pinterest · LinkedIn

○ ○ ○ ○ ○ ○ ○ ○

Account Name : _____

Name : _____

Address : _____

_____

Payment Methods

○ Cash on delivery   Amount

○ Check payment   _____

○ Direct bank transfer   Date Paid

○ PayPal   _____

Order Number : _____

Date of order : _____

Ship date : _____

Shipping carrier : _____

Tracking ID : _____

Delivered : _____

Special option

○ Samples sent

○ Gift Message

_____

_____

Product No.	Description	Qty.	Total

Notes:			
	Total	
	Product Cost	
	Postage Cost	
	Tax	
	Profit	

Social Media Icons

(🐦) (📷) (f) (👻) (▶) (v) (P) (in)

○ ○ ○ ○ ○ ○ ○ ○

Account Name : _____

Name : _____

Address : _____

_____

Payment Methods

○ Cash on delivery   Amount

○ Check payment   _____

○ Direct bank transfer   Date Paid

○ PayPal   _____

Order Number : _____

Date of order : _____

Ship date : _____

Shipping carrier : _____

Tracking ID : _____

Delivered : _____

Special option

○ Samples sent

○ Gift Message

_____

_____

Product No.	Description	Qty.	Total

Notes:		
	Total	
	Product Cost	
	Postage Cost	
	Tax	
	Profit	

Twitter ⭘ Instagram ⭘ Facebook ⭘ Snapchat ⭘ YouTube ⭘ Vimeo ⭘ Pinterest ⭘ LinkedIn ⭘

Account Name : _____

Name : _____

Address : _____

_____

Payment Methods

⭘ Cash on delivery   Amount

⭘ Check payment   _____

⭘ Direct bank transfer   Date Paid

⭘ PayPal   _____

Order Number : _____

Date of order : _____

Ship date : _____

Shipping carrier : _____

Tracking ID : _____

Delivered : _____

Special option

⭘ Samples sent

⭘ Gift Message

_____

_____

Product No.	Description	Qty.	Total

Notes:		
	Total	
	Product Cost	
	Postage Cost	
	Tax	
	Profit	

Account Name : _____

Name : _____

Address : _____

_____

Order Number : _____

Date of order : _____

Ship date : _____

Shipping carrier : _____

Tracking ID : _____

Delivered : _____

Payment Methods

O Cash on delivery   Amount

O Check payment   _____

O Direct bank transfer   Date Paid

O PayPal   _____

Special option

O Samples sent

O Gift Message

_____

_____

Product No.	Description	Qty.	Total

Notes:		
	Total	
	Product Cost	
	Postage Cost	
	Tax	
	Profit	

Account Name : _____

Name : _____

Address : _____

_____

Payment Methods

○ Cash on delivery   Amount

○ Check payment   _____

○ Direct bank transfer   Date Paid

○ PayPal   _____

Order Number : _____

Date of order : _____

Ship date : _____

Shipping carrier : _____

Tracking ID : _____

Delivered : _____

Special option

○ Samples sent

○ Gift Message

_____

_____

Product No.	Description	Qty.	Total

Notes:		
	Total	
	Product Cost	
	Postage Cost	
	Tax	
	Profit	

Account Name : _____

Name : _____

Address : _____

_____

Order Number : _____

Date of order : _____

Ship date : _____

Shipping carrier : _____

Tracking ID : _____

Delivered : _____

Payment Methods

O Cash on delivery   Amount

O Check payment   _____

O Direct bank transfer   Date Paid

O PayPal   _____

Special option

O Samples sent

O Gift Message

_____

_____

Product No.	Description	Qty.	Total

Notes:			
		Total	
		Product Cost	
		Postage Cost	
		Tax	
		Profit	

Account Information

Account Name : _____

Name : _____

Address : _____

_____

Payment Methods

- ○ Cash on delivery   Amount
- ○ Check payment   _____
- ○ Direct bank transfer   Date Paid
- ○ PayPal   _____

Order Details

Order Number : _____

Date of order : _____

Ship date : _____

Shipping carrier : _____

Tracking ID : _____

Delivered : _____

Special option

- ○ Samples sent
- ○ Gift Message

_____

_____

Product No.	Description	Qty.	Total

Notes:

	Total	
	Product Cost	
	Postage Cost	
	Tax	
	Profit	

Account Name : _____

Name : _____

Address : _____

_____

Order Number : _____

Date of order : _____

Ship date : _____

Shipping carrier : _____

Tracking ID : _____

Delivered : _____

Payment Methods

O Cash on delivery   Amount

O Check payment   _____

O Direct bank transfer   Date Paid

O PayPal   _____

Special option

O Samples sent

O Gift Message

_____

_____

Product No.	Description	Qty.	Total

Notes:		Total	
		Product Cost	
		Postage Cost	
		Tax	
		Profit	

Account Name : _____

Name : _____

Address : _____

_____

Payment Methods

- ○ Cash on delivery
- ○ Check payment
- ○ Direct bank transfer
- ○ PayPal

Amount

_____

Date Paid

_____

Order Number : _____

Date of order : _____

Ship date : _____

Shipping carrier : _____

Tracking ID : _____

Delivered : _____

Special option

- ○ Samples sent
- ○ Gift Message

_____

_____

Product No.	Description	Qty.	Total

Notes:

Total	
Product Cost	
Postage Cost	
Tax	
Profit	

Account Name : _____

Name : _____

Address : _____

_____

Payment Methods

- O Cash on delivery   Amount
- O Check payment   _____
- O Direct bank transfer   Date Paid
- O PayPal   _____

Order Number : _____

Date of order : _____

Ship date : _____

Shipping carrier : _____

Tracking ID : _____

Delivered : _____

Special option

- O Samples sent
- O Gift Message

_____

_____

Product No.	Description	Qty.	Total

Notes:		Total	
		Product Cost	
		Postage Cost	
		Tax	
		Profit	

Account Name : _____

Name : _____

Address : _____

_____

Payment Methods

○ Cash on delivery   Amount

○ Check payment   _____

○ Direct bank transfer   Date Paid

○ PayPal   _____

Order Number : _____

Date of order : _____

Ship date : _____

Shipping carrier : _____

Tracking ID : _____

Delivered : _____

Special option

○ Samples sent

○ Gift Message

_____

_____

Product No.	Description	Qty.	Total

Notes:		
	Total	
	Product Cost	
	Postage Cost	
	Tax	
	Profit	

Account Name : _____

Name : _____

Address : _____

_____

Payment Methods

○ Cash on delivery   Amount

○ Check payment   _____

○ Direct bank transfer   Date Paid

○ PayPal   _____

Order Number : _____

Date of order : _____

Ship date : _____

Shipping carrier : _____

Tracking ID : _____

Delivered : _____

Special option

○ Samples sent

○ Gift Message

_____

_____

Product No.	Description	Qty.	Total

Notes:

Total	
Product Cost	
Postage Cost	
Tax	
Profit	

Social Media Icons

○ ○ ○ ○ ○ ○ ○ ○

Account Name : _____

Name : _____

Address : _____

_____

Payment Methods

○ Cash on delivery   Amount

○ Check payment   _____

○ Direct bank transfer   Date Paid

○ PayPal   _____

Order Number : _____

Date of order : _____

Ship date : _____

Shipping carrier : _____

Tracking ID : _____

Delivered : _____

Special option

○ Samples sent

○ Gift Message

_____

_____

Product No.	Description	Qty.	Total

Notes:

	Total	
	Product Cost	
	Postage Cost	
	Tax	
	Profit	

Social Media Icons

(🐦) (📷) (f) (👻) (▶) (v) (𝓟) (in)

○ ○ ○ ○ ○ ○ ○ ○

Account Name : _____

Name : _____

Address : _____

_____

Payment Methods

○ Cash on delivery   Amount

○ Check payment   _____

○ Direct bank transfer   Date Paid

○ PayPal   _____

Order Number : _____

Date of order : _____

Ship date : _____

Shipping carrier : _____

Tracking ID : _____

Delivered : _____

Special option

○ Samples sent

○ Gift Message

_____

_____

Product No.	Description	Qty.	Total

Notes:

	Total	
	Product Cost	
	Postage Cost	
	Tax	
	Profit	

| Twitter | Instagram | Facebook | Snapchat | YouTube | Vimeo | Pinterest | LinkedIn |
| ○ | ○ | ○ | ○ | ○ | ○ | ○ | ○ |

Account Name : _____

Name : _____

Address : _____

_____

Payment Methods

- O Cash on delivery   Amount
- O Check payment   _____
- O Direct bank transfer   Date Paid
- O PayPal   _____

Order Number : _____

Date of order : _____

Ship date : _____

Shipping carrier : _____

Tracking ID : _____

Delivered : _____

Special option

- O Samples sent
- O Gift Message

_____

_____

Product No.	Description	Qty.	Total

Notes:

Total	
Product Cost	
Postage Cost	
Tax	
Profit	

Account Name : _____

Name : _____

Address : _____

_____

Order Number : _____

Date of order : _____

Ship date : _____

Shipping carrier : _____

Tracking ID : _____

Delivered : _____

O Cash on delivery   Amount

O Check payment   _____

O Direct bank transfer   Date Paid

O PayPal   _____

Special option

O Samples sent

O Gift Message

_____

_____

Product No.	Description	Qty.	Total

Notes:

Total		
Product Cost		
Postage Cost		
Tax		
Profit		

Account Name : _____

Name : _____

Address : _____

_____

Order Number : _____

Date of order : _____

Ship date : _____

Shipping carrier : _____

Tracking ID : _____

Delivered : _____

Payment Methods

O Cash on delivery   Amount

O Check payment   _____

O Direct bank transfer   Date Paid

O PayPal   _____

Special option

O Samples sent

O Gift Message

_____

_____

Product No.	Description	Qty.	Total

Notes:

Total	
Product Cost	
Postage Cost	
Tax	
Profit	

Account Name : _____

Name : _____

Address : _____

_____

Payment Methods

○ Cash on delivery   Amount

○ Check payment   _____

○ Direct bank transfer   Date Paid

○ PayPal   _____

Order Number : _____

Date of order : _____

Ship date : _____

Shipping carrier : _____

Tracking ID : _____

Delivered : _____

Special option

○ Samples sent

○ Gift Message

_____

_____

Product No.	Description	Qty.	Total

Notes:		
	Total	
	Product Cost	
	Postage Cost	
	Tax	
	Profit	

Account Name : _____

Name : _____

Address : _____

_____

Order Number : _____

Date of order : _____

Ship date : _____

Shipping carrier : _____

Tracking ID : _____

Delivered : _____

Payment Methods

- ○ Cash on delivery   Amount
- ○ Check payment   _____
- ○ Direct bank transfer   Date Paid
- ○ PayPal   _____

Special option

- ○ Samples sent
- ○ Gift Message

_____

_____

Product No.	Description	Qty.	Total

Notes:

	Total	
	Product Cost	
	Postage Cost	
	Tax	
	Profit	

Account Name : _____

Name : _____

Address : _____

_____

Order Number : _____

Date of order : _____

Ship date : _____

Shipping carrier : _____

Tracking ID : _____

Delivered : _____

Payment Methods

○ Cash on delivery

○ Check payment

○ Direct bank transfer

○ PayPal

Amount

_____

Date Paid

_____

Special option

○ Samples sent

○ Gift Message

_____

_____

Product No.	Description	Qty.	Total

Notes:

Total	
Product Cost	
Postage Cost	
Tax	
Profit	

Account Name : _____

Name : _____

Address : _____

_____

Payment Methods

O Cash on delivery   Amount

O Check payment   _____

O Direct bank transfer   Date Paid

O PayPal   _____

Order Number : _____

Date of order : _____

Ship date : _____

Shipping carrier : _____

Tracking ID : _____

Delivered : _____

Special option

O Samples sent

O Gift Message

_____

_____

Product No.	Description	Qty.	Total

Notes:			
	Total	
	Product Cost	
	Postage Cost	
	Tax	
	Profit	

Account Name : _____

Name : _____

Address : _____

_____

Order Number : _____

Date of order : _____

Ship date : _____

Shipping carrier : _____

Tracking ID : _____

Delivered : _____

Payment Methods

○ Cash on delivery   Amount

○ Check payment   _____

○ Direct bank transfer   Date Paid

○ PayPal   _____

Special option

○ Samples sent

○ Gift Message

_____

_____

Product No.	Description	Qty.	Total

Notes:		Total	
		Product Cost	
		Postage Cost	
		Tax	
		Profit	

Account Name : _____

Name : _____

Address : _____

_____

Order Number : _____

Date of order : _____

Ship date : _____

Shipping carrier : _____

Tracking ID : _____

Delivered : _____

Payment Methods

O Cash on delivery   Amount

O Check payment   _____

O Direct bank transfer   Date Paid

O PayPal   _____

Special option

O Samples sent

O Gift Message

_____

_____

Product No.	Description	Qty.	Total

Notes:

	Total	
	Product Cost	
	Postage Cost	
	Tax	
	Profit	

Order Details

Account Name : _____	Order Number : _____	
Name : _____	Date of order : _____	
Address : _____	Ship date : _____	
_____	Shipping carrier : _____	

Account Name : _____

Name : _____

Address : _____
_____

Payment Methods

- ○ Cash on delivery   Amount
- ○ Check payment   _____
- ○ Direct bank transfer   Date Paid
- ○ PayPal   _____

Order Number : _____

Date of order : _____

Ship date : _____

Shipping carrier : _____

Tracking ID : _____

Delivered : _____

Special option

- ○ Samples sent
- ○ Gift Message

_____
_____

Product No.	Description	Qty.	Total

Notes:		
	Total	
	Product Cost	
	Postage Cost	
	Tax	
	Profit	

Account Name : _____

Name : _____

Address : _____

_____

O Cash on delivery   Amount

O Check payment   _____

O Direct bank transfer   Date Paid

O PayPal   _____

Order Number : _____

Date of order : _____

Ship date : _____

Shipping carrier : _____

Tracking ID : _____

Delivered : _____

Special option

O Samples sent

O Gift Message

_____

_____

Product No.	Description	Qty.	Total

Notes:			
		Total	
		Product Cost	
		Postage Cost	
		Tax	
		Profit	

Account Name : _____

Name : _____

Address : _____

_____

Payment Methods

- ○ Cash on delivery   Amount
- ○ Check payment   _____
- ○ Direct bank transfer   Date Paid
- ○ PayPal   _____

Order Number : _____

Date of order : _____

Ship date : _____

Shipping carrier : _____

Tracking ID : _____

Delivered : _____

Special option

- ○ Samples sent
- ○ Gift Message

_____

_____

Product No.	Description	Qty.	Total

Notes:

Total	
Product Cost	
Postage Cost	
Tax	
Profit	

○ ○ ○ ○ ○ ○ ○ ○

Account Name : _____

Name : _____

Address : _____

_____

Order Number : _____

Date of order : _____

Ship date : _____

Shipping carrier : _____

Tracking ID : _____

Delivered : _____

Payment Methods

○ Cash on delivery   Amount

○ Check payment   _____

○ Direct bank transfer   Date Paid

○ PayPal   _____

Special option

○ Samples sent

○ Gift Message

_____

_____

Product No.	Description	Qty.	Total
Notes:		Total	
		Product Cost	
		Postage Cost	
		Tax	
		Profit	

Account Name : _____

Name : _____

Address : _____

_____

Payment Methods

- ○ Cash on delivery   Amount
- ○ Check payment _____
- ○ Direct bank transfer   Date Paid
- ○ PayPal _____

Order Number : _____

Date of order : _____

Ship date : _____

Shipping carrier : _____

Tracking ID : _____

Delivered : _____

Special option

- ○ Samples sent
- ○ Gift Message

_____

_____

Product No.	Description	Qty.	Total

Notes:

	Total	
	Product Cost	
	Postage Cost	
	Tax	
	Profit	

Account Name : _____

Name : _____

Address : _____

_____

Order Number : _____

Date of order : _____

Ship date : _____

Shipping carrier : _____

Tracking ID : _____

Delivered : _____

| Payment Methods | | | Special option | |

- O Cash on delivery   Amount
- O Check payment   _____
- O Direct bank transfer   Date Paid
- O PayPal   _____

- O Samples sent
- O Gift Message

_____

_____

Product No.	Description	Qty.	Total

Notes:

Total	
Product Cost	
Postage Cost	
Tax	
Profit	

Account Name : _____

Name : _____

Address : _____

_____

Order Number : _____

Date of order : _____

Ship date : _____

Shipping carrier : _____

Tracking ID : _____

Delivered : _____

Payment Methods

○ Cash on delivery   Amount

○ Check payment   _____

○ Direct bank transfer   Date Paid

○ PayPal   _____

Special option

○ Samples sent

○ Gift Message

_____

_____

Product No.	Description	Qty.	Total

Notes:

Total	
Product Cost	.
Postage Cost	
Tax	
Profit	

Account Name : _____

Name : _____

Address : _____

_____

Order Number : _____

Date of order : _____

Ship date : _____

Shipping carrier : _____

Tracking ID : _____

Delivered : _____

Payment Methods

- ○ Cash on delivery   Amount
- ○ Check payment   _____
- ○ Direct bank transfer   Date Paid
- ○ PayPal   _____

Special option

- ○ Samples sent
- ○ Gift Message

_____

_____

Product No.	Description	Qty.	Total

Notes:

	Total	
	Product Cost	
	Postage Cost	
	Tax	
	Profit	

Account Name : _____

Name : _____

Address : _____

_____

Payment Methods

○ Cash on delivery   Amount

○ Check payment   _____

○ Direct bank transfer   Date Paid

○ PayPal   _____

Order Number : _____

Date of order : _____

Ship date : _____

Shipping carrier : _____

Tracking ID : _____

Delivered : _____

Special option

○ Samples sent

○ Gift Message

_____

_____

Product No.	Description	Qty.	Total

Notes:

Total	
Product Cost	
Postage Cost	
Tax	
Profit	

Account Name : _____

Name : _____

Address : _____

_____

Order Number : _____

Date of order : _____

Ship date : _____

Shipping carrier : _____

Tracking ID : _____

Delivered : _____

Payment Methods

O Cash on delivery   Amount

O Check payment   _____

O Direct bank transfer   Date Paid

O PayPal   _____

Special option

O Samples sent

O Gift Message

_____

_____

Product No.	Description	Qty.	Total

Notes:		
	Total	
	Product Cost	
	Postage Cost	
	Tax	
	Profit	

Account Name : _____

Name : _____

Address : _____

_____

Order Number : _____

Date of order : _____

Ship date : _____

Shipping carrier : _____

Tracking ID : _____

Delivered : _____

Payment Methods

○ Cash on delivery   Amount

○ Check payment   _____

○ Direct bank transfer   Date Paid

○ PayPal   _____

Special option

○ Samples sent

○ Gift Message

_____

_____

Product No.	Description	Qty.	Total

Notes:	Total	
	Product Cost	
	Postage Cost	
	Tax	
	Profit	

Account Details

🐦 📷 f 👻 ▶ Ⓥ Ⓟ in
○ ○ ○ ○ ○ ○ ○ ○

Account Name : _____

Name : _____

Address : _____

_____

Payment Methods

○ Cash on delivery   Amount

○ Check payment   _____

○ Direct bank transfer   Date Paid

○ PayPal   _____

Order Number : _____

Date of order : _____

Ship date : _____

Shipping carrier : _____

Tracking ID : _____

Delivered : _____

Special option

○ Samples sent

○ Gift Message

_____

_____

Product No.	Description	Qty.	Total

Notes:

	Total	
	Product Cost	
	Postage Cost	
	Tax	
	Profit	

Account Name : _____

Name : _____

Address : _____

_____

Order Number : _____

Date of order : _____

Ship date : _____

Shipping carrier : _____

Tracking ID : _____

Delivered : _____

Payment Methods

- ○ Cash on delivery   Amount
- ○ Check payment   _____
- ○ Direct bank transfer   Date Paid
- ○ PayPal   _____

Special option

- ○ Samples sent
- ○ Gift Message

_____

_____

Product No.	Description	Qty.	Total

Notes:

Total	
Product Cost	
Postage Cost	
Tax	
Profit	

<table>
<tr><td colspan="2">

Account Name : _____

Name : _____

Address : _____

_____

Payment Methods

- ○ Cash on delivery   Amount
- ○ Check payment   _____
- ○ Direct bank transfer   Date Paid
- ○ PayPal   _____

</td><td colspan="2">

Order Number : _____

Date of order : _____

Ship date : _____

Shipping carrier : _____

Tracking ID : _____

Delivered : _____

Special option

- ○ Samples sent
- ○ Gift Message

_____

_____

</td></tr>
</table>

Product No.	Description	Qty.	Total
Notes:		Total	
		Product Cost	
		Postage Cost	
		Tax	
		Profit	

Social Media Icons

Twitter	Instagram	Facebook	Snapchat	YouTube	Vimeo	Pinterest	LinkedIn
○	○	○	○	○	○	○	○

Account Name : _____

Name : _____

Address : _____

_____

Payment Methods

○ Cash on delivery   Amount

○ Check payment   _____

○ Direct bank transfer   Date Paid

○ PayPal   _____

Order Number : _____

Date of order : _____

Ship date : _____

Shipping carrier : _____

Tracking ID : _____

Delivered : _____

Special option

○ Samples sent

○ Gift Message

_____

_____

Product No.	Description	Qty.	Total

Notes:		
	Total	
	Product Cost	
	Postage Cost	
	Tax	
	Profit	

Account Name : _____

Name : _____

Address : _____

_____

Order Number : _____

Date of order : _____

Ship date : _____

Shipping carrier : _____

Tracking ID : _____

Delivered : _____

Payment Methods

O Cash on delivery   Amount

O Check payment   _____

O Direct bank transfer   Date Paid

O PayPal   _____

Special option

O Samples sent

O Gift Message

_____

_____

Product No.	Description	Qty.	Total
Notes:		Total	
		Product Cost	
		Postage Cost	
		Tax	
		Profit	

Account Name : _____

Name : _____

Address : _____

_____

Payment Methods

○ Cash on delivery   Amount

○ Check payment   _____

○ Direct bank transfer   Date Paid

○ PayPal   _____

Order Number : _____

Date of order : _____

Ship date : _____

Shipping carrier : _____

Tracking ID : _____

Delivered : _____

Special option

○ Samples sent

○ Gift Message

_____

_____

Product No.	Description	Qty.	Total

Notes:

Total	
Product Cost	
Postage Cost	
Tax	
Profit	

Account Name : _____

Name : _____

Address : _____

_____

Payment Methods

○ Cash on delivery   Amount

○ Check payment   _____

○ Direct bank transfer   Date Paid

○ PayPal   _____

Order Number : _____

Date of order : _____

Ship date : _____

Shipping carrier : _____

Tracking ID : _____

Delivered : _____

Special option

○ Samples sent

○ Gift Message

_____

_____

Product No.	Description	Qty.	Total

Notes:		Total	
		Product Cost	
		Postage Cost	
		Tax	
		Profit	

Social Media Icons

Account Name : _____

Name : _____

Address : _____

_____

Payment Methods

- ○ Cash on delivery   Amount
- ○ Check payment   _____
- ○ Direct bank transfer   Date Paid
- ○ PayPal   _____

Order Number : _____

Date of order : _____

Ship date : _____

Shipping carrier : _____

Tracking ID : _____

Delivered : _____

Special option

- ○ Samples sent
- ○ Gift Message

_____

_____

Product No.	Description	Qty.	Total

Notes:

Total	
Product Cost	
Postage Cost	
Tax	
Profit	

🐦	📷	f	👻	▶	v	📌	in
○	○	○	○	○	○	○	○

Account Name : _____

Name : _____

Address : _____

_____

Order Number : _____

Date of order : _____

Ship date : _____

Shipping carrier : _____

Tracking ID : _____

Delivered : _____

Payment Methods

○ Cash on delivery   Amount

○ Check payment   _____

○ Direct bank transfer   Date Paid

○ PayPal   _____

Special option

○ Samples sent

○ Gift Message

_____

_____

Product No.	Description	Qty.	Total

Notes:		
	Total	
	Product Cost	
	Postage Cost	
	Tax	
	Profit	

Order Number : _____

Date of order : _____

Ship date : _____

Shipping carrier : _____

Tracking ID : _____

Delivered : _____

Special option

○ Samples sent

○ Gift Message

_____

_____

Product No.	Description	Qty.	Total

Notes:	Total	
	Product Cost	
	Postage Cost	
	Tax	
	Profit	

○ 🐦 ○ 📷 ○ f ○ 👻 ○ ▶ ○ Ⓥ ○ ℗ ○ in
○ ○ ○ ○ ○ ○ ○ ○

Account Name : _____

Name : _____

Address : _____

_____

Order Number : _____

Date of order : _____

Ship date : _____

Shipping carrier : _____

Tracking ID : _____

Delivered : _____

Payment Methods

○ Cash on delivery   Amount

○ Check payment   _____

○ Direct bank transfer   Date Paid

○ PayPal   _____

Special option

○ Samples sent

○ Gift Message

_____

_____

Product No.	Description	Qty.	Total
Notes:		Total	
		Product Cost	
		Postage Cost	
		Tax	
		Profit	

Account Name : _____

Name : _____

Address : _____

_____

Order Number : _____

Date of order : _____

Ship date : _____

Shipping carrier : _____

Tracking ID : _____

Delivered : _____

Payment Methods

- O Cash on delivery   Amount
- O Check payment   _____
- O Direct bank transfer   Date Paid
- O PayPal   _____

Special option

- O Samples sent
- O Gift Message

_____

_____

Product No.	Description	Qty.	Total

Notes:

	Total	
	Product Cost	
	Postage Cost	
	Tax	
	Profit	

Account Info

(ⓣ) (ⓘ) (ⓕ) (ⓢ) (▶) (ⓥ) (ⓟ) (in)

○ ○ ○ ○ ○ ○ ○ ○

Account Name : _____

Name : _____

Address : _____

_____

Payment Methods

○ Cash on delivery   Amount

○ Check payment   _____

○ Direct bank transfer   Date Paid

○ PayPal   _____

Order Number : _____

Date of order : _____

Ship date : _____

Shipping carrier : _____

Tracking ID : _____

Delivered : _____

Special option

○ Samples sent

○ Gift Message

_____

_____

Product No.	Description	Qty.	Total

Notes:			
		Total	
		Product Cost	
		Postage Cost	
		Tax	
		Profit	

Account Name : _____

Name : _____

Address : _____

_____

Payment Methods

○ Cash on delivery   Amount

○ Check payment   _____

○ Direct bank transfer   Date Paid

○ PayPal   _____

Order Number : _____

Date of order : _____

Ship date : _____

Shipping carrier : _____

Tracking ID : _____

Delivered : _____

Special option

○ Samples sent

○ Gift Message

_____

_____

Product No.	Description	Qty.	Total

Notes:

Total	
Product Cost	
Postage Cost	
Tax	
Profit	

Account Name : _____

Name : _____

Address : _____

_____

Order Number : _____

Date of order : _____

Ship date : _____

Shipping carrier : _____

Tracking ID : _____

Delivered : _____

Payment Methods

- O Cash on delivery
- O Check payment
- O Direct bank transfer
- O PayPal

Amount

_____

Date Paid

_____

Special option

- O Samples sent
- O Gift Message

_____

_____

Product No.	Description	Qty.	Total

Notes:

	Total	
	Product Cost	
	Postage Cost	
	Tax	
	Profit	

Account Name : _____

Name : _____

Address : _____

_____

Order Number : _____

Date of order : _____

Ship date : _____

Shipping carrier : _____

Tracking ID : _____

Delivered : _____

Payment Methods

○ Cash on delivery   Amount

○ Check payment   _____

○ Direct bank transfer   Date Paid

○ PayPal   _____

Special option

○ Samples sent

○ Gift Message

_____

_____

Product No.	Description	Qty.	Total

Notes:			
	Total	
	Product Cost	
	Postage Cost	
	Tax	
	Profit	

			Order Number : _____

Account Name : _____

Name : _____

Address : _____

_____

Order Number : _____

Date of order : _____

Ship date : _____

Shipping carrier : _____

Tracking ID : _____

Delivered : _____

Payment Methods

O Cash on delivery   Amount

O Check payment   _____

O Direct bank transfer   Date Paid

O PayPal   _____

Special option

O Samples sent

O Gift Message

_____

_____

Product No.	Description	Qty.	Total

Notes:		Total	
		Product Cost	
		Postage Cost	
		Tax	
		Profit	

Account Name : _____

Name : _____

Address : _____

_____

Payment Methods

- ○ Cash on delivery   Amount
- ○ Check payment   _____
- ○ Direct bank transfer   Date Paid
- ○ PayPal   _____

Order Number : _____

Date of order : _____

Ship date : _____

Shipping carrier : _____

Tracking ID : _____

Delivered : _____

Special option

- ○ Samples sent
- ○ Gift Message

_____

_____

Product No.	Description	Qty.	Total
Notes:		Total	
		Product Cost	
		Postage Cost	
		Tax	
		Profit	

Account Name : _____

Name : _____

Address : _____

_____

Payment Methods

O Cash on delivery   Amount

O Check payment   _____

O Direct bank transfer   Date Paid

O PayPal   _____

Order Number : _____

Date of order : _____

Ship date : _____

Shipping carrier : _____

Tracking ID : _____

Delivered : _____

Special option

O Samples sent

O Gift Message

_____

_____

Product No.	Description	Qty.	Total

Notes:

Total	
Product Cost	
Postage Cost	
Tax	
Profit	

Account Name : _____

Name : _____

Address : _____

_____

Payment Methods

O Cash on delivery   Amount

O Check payment   _____

O Direct bank transfer   Date Paid

O PayPal   _____

Order Number : _____

Date of order : _____

Ship date : _____

Shipping carrier : _____

Tracking ID : _____

Delivered : _____

Special option

O Samples sent

O Gift Message

_____

_____

Product No.	Description	Qty.	Total

Notes:

Total	
Product Cost	
Postage Cost	
Tax	
Profit	

Account Name : _____

Name : _____

Address : _____

_____

| Payment Methods |

- O Cash on delivery   Amount
- O Check payment   _____
- O Direct bank transfer   Date Paid
- O PayPal   _____

Order Number : _____

Date of order : _____

Ship date : _____

Shipping carrier : _____

Tracking ID : _____

Delivered : _____

| Special option |

- O Samples sent
- O Gift Message

_____

_____

Product No.	Description	Qty.	Total

Notes:

	Total	
	Product Cost	
	Postage Cost	
	Tax	
	Profit	

Account Name : _____

Name : _____

Address : _____

_____

Order Number : _____

Date of order : _____

Ship date : _____

Shipping carrier : _____

Tracking ID : _____

Delivered : _____

Payment Methods

- ○ Cash on delivery   Amount
- ○ Check payment   _____
- ○ Direct bank transfer   Date Paid
- ○ PayPal   _____

Special option

- ○ Samples sent
- ○ Gift Message

_____

_____

Product No.	Description	Qty.	Total

Notes:		Total	
		Product Cost	
		Postage Cost	
		Tax	
		Profit	

| | Twitter | Instagram | Facebook | Snapchat | YouTube | Vimeo | Pinterest | LinkedIn |
| O | O | O | O | O | O | O | O |

Account Name : _____

Name : _____

Address : _____

_____

Payment Methods

- O Cash on delivery   Amount
- O Check payment   _____
- O Direct bank transfer   Date Paid
- O PayPal   _____

Order Number : _____

Date of order : _____

Ship date : _____

Shipping carrier : _____

Tracking ID : _____

Delivered : _____

Special option

- O Samples sent
- O Gift Message

_____

_____

Product No.	Description	Qty.	Total

Notes:

Total		
Product Cost		
Postage Cost		
Tax		
Profit		

Account Name : _____

Name : _____

Address : _____

_____

Order Number : _____

Date of order : _____

Ship date : _____

Shipping carrier : _____

Tracking ID : _____

Delivered : _____

Payment Methods

- O Cash on delivery   Amount
- O Check payment   _____
- O Direct bank transfer   Date Paid
- O PayPal   _____

Special option

- O Samples sent
- O Gift Message

_____

_____

Product No.	Description	Qty.	Total

Notes:		Total	
		Product Cost	
		Postage Cost	
		Tax	
		Profit	

Account Name : _____

Name : _____

Address : _____

_____

Payment Methods

- O Cash on delivery   Amount
- O Check payment   _____
- O Direct bank transfer   Date Paid
- O PayPal   _____

Order Number : _____

Date of order : _____

Ship date : _____

Shipping carrier : _____

Tracking ID : _____

Delivered : _____

Special option

- O Samples sent
- O Gift Message

_____

_____

Product No.	Description	Qty.	Total

Notes:

Total	
Product Cost	
Postage Cost	
Tax	
Profit	

Account

Account Name : _____

Name : _____

Address : _____

_____

Order Number : _____

Date of order : _____

Ship date : _____

Shipping carrier : _____

Tracking ID : _____

Delivered : _____

Special option

- ○ Samples sent
- ○ Gift Message

_____

_____

Product No.	Description	Qty.	Total

Notes:		Total	
		Product Cost	
		Postage Cost	
		Tax	
		Profit	

Account Name : _____

Name : _____

Address : _____

_____

Order Number : _____

Date of order : _____

Ship date : _____

Shipping carrier : _____

Tracking ID : _____

Delivered : _____

Payment Methods

O Cash on delivery   Amount

O Check payment   _____

O Direct bank transfer   Date Paid

O PayPal   _____

Special option

O Samples sent

O Gift Message

_____

_____

Product No.	Description	Qty.	Total

Notes:

Total	
Product Cost	
Postage Cost	
Tax	
Profit	

Account Name : _____

Name : _____

Address : _____

_____

Order Number : _____

Date of order : _____

Ship date : _____

Shipping carrier : _____

Tracking ID : _____

Delivered : _____

Payment Methods

○ Cash on delivery   Amount

○ Check payment   _____

○ Direct bank transfer   Date Paid

○ PayPal   _____

Special option

○ Samples sent

○ Gift Message

_____

_____

Product No.	Description	Qty.	Total

Notes:		
	Total	
	Product Cost	
	Postage Cost	
	Tax	
	Profit	

Account Name : _____

Name : _____

Address : _____

_____

Payment Methods

- O Cash on delivery   Amount
- O Check payment   _____
- O Direct bank transfer   Date Paid
- O PayPal   _____

Order Number : _____

Date of order : _____

Ship date : _____

Shipping carrier : _____

Tracking ID : _____

Delivered : _____

Special option

- O Samples sent
- O Gift Message

_____

_____

Product No.	Description	Qty.	Total

Notes:

Total	
Product Cost	
Postage Cost	
Tax	
Profit	

Account Name : _____

Name : _____

Address : _____

_____

Payment Methods

○ Cash on delivery   Amount

○ Check payment   _____

○ Direct bank transfer   Date Paid

○ PayPal   _____

Order Number : _____

Date of order : _____

Ship date : _____

Shipping carrier : _____

Tracking ID : _____

Delivered : _____

Special option

○ Samples sent

○ Gift Message

_____

_____

Product No.	Description	Qty.	Total

Notes:		
	Total	
	Product Cost	
	Postage Cost	
	Tax	
	Profit	

Social Media Icons

○ ○ ○ ○ ○ ○ ○ ○

Account Name : _____

Name : _____

Address : _____

_____

Payment Methods

- ○ Cash on delivery   Amount
- ○ Check payment   _____
- ○ Direct bank transfer   Date Paid
- ○ PayPal   _____

Order Number : _____

Date of order : _____

Ship date : _____

Shipping carrier : _____

Tracking ID : _____

Delivered : _____

Special option

- ○ Samples sent
- ○ Gift Message

_____

_____

Product No.	Description	Qty.	Total

Notes:

Total	
Product Cost	
Postage Cost	
Tax	
Profit	

Account Information

Account Name : _____

Name : _____

Address : _____

_____

Payment Methods

- ○ Cash on delivery   Amount
- ○ Check payment   _____
- ○ Direct bank transfer   Date Paid
- ○ PayPal   _____

Order Number : _____

Date of order : _____

Ship date : _____

Shipping carrier : _____

Tracking ID : _____

Delivered : _____

Special option

- ○ Samples sent
- ○ Gift Message

_____

_____

Product No.	Description	Qty.	Total

Notes:

Total	
Product Cost	
Postage Cost	
Tax	
Profit	

Account Name : _____

Name : _____

Address : _____

_____

Payment Methods

- ◯ Cash on delivery   Amount
- ◯ Check payment   _____
- ◯ Direct bank transfer   Date Paid
- ◯ PayPal   _____

Order Number : _____

Date of order : _____

Ship date : _____

Shipping carrier : _____

Tracking ID : _____

Delivered : _____

Special option

- ◯ Samples sent
- ◯ Gift Message

_____

_____

Product No.	Description	Qty.	Total

Notes:

Total	
Product Cost	
Postage Cost	
Tax	
Profit	

Account Details

🐦	📷	f	👻	▶	v	𝓟	in
○	○	○	○	○	○	○	○

Account Name : _____

Name : _____

Address : _____

_____

Payment Methods

- ○ Cash on delivery   Amount
- ○ Check payment   _____
- ○ Direct bank transfer   Date Paid
- ○ PayPal   _____

Order Number : _____

Date of order : _____

Ship date : _____

Shipping carrier : _____

Tracking ID : _____

Delivered : _____

Special option

- ○ Samples sent
- ○ Gift Message

_____

_____

Product No.	Description	Qty.	Total

Notes:		Total	
		Product Cost	
		Postage Cost	
		Tax	
		Profit	

Account Name : _____

Name : _____

Address : _____

_____

Order Number : _____

Date of order : _____

Ship date : _____

Shipping carrier : _____

Tracking ID : _____

Delivered : _____

Payment Methods

O Cash on delivery   Amount

O Check payment   _____

O Direct bank transfer   Date Paid

O PayPal   _____

Special option

O Samples sent

O Gift Message

_____

_____

Product No.	Description	Qty.	Total

Notes:

Total		
Product Cost		
Postage Cost		
Tax		
Profit		

Account Details

Account Name : _____

Name : _____

Address : _____

_____

Payment Methods

- ○ Cash on delivery   Amount
- ○ Check payment   _____
- ○ Direct bank transfer   Date Paid
- ○ PayPal   _____

Order Number : _____

Date of order : _____

Ship date : _____

Shipping carrier : _____

Tracking ID : _____

Delivered : _____

Special option

- ○ Samples sent
- ○ Gift Message

_____

_____

Product No.	Description	Qty.	Total
Notes:		Total	
		Product Cost	
		Postage Cost	
		Tax	
		Profit	

Account Name : _____

Name : _____

Address : _____

_____

O Cash on delivery   Amount

O Check payment   _____

O Direct bank transfer   Date Paid

O PayPal   _____

Order Number : _____

Date of order : _____

Ship date : _____

Shipping carrier : _____

Tracking ID : _____

Delivered : _____

Special option

O Samples sent

O Gift Message

_____

_____

Product No.	Description	Qty.	Total

Notes:		Total	
		Product Cost	
		Postage Cost	
		Tax	
		Profit	

Twitter ⃝ Instagram ⃝ Facebook ⃝ Snapchat ⃝ YouTube ⃝ Vimeo ⃝ Pinterest ⃝ LinkedIn ⃝

Account Name : _____

Name : _____

Address : _____

_____

Payment Methods

○ Cash on delivery   Amount

○ Check payment   _____

○ Direct bank transfer   Date Paid

○ PayPal   _____

Order Number : _____

Date of order : _____

Ship date : _____

Shipping carrier : _____

Tracking ID : _____

Delivered : _____

Special option

○ Samples sent

○ Gift Message

_____

_____

Product No.	Description	Qty.	Total

Notes:			
		Total	
		Product Cost	
		Postage Cost	
		Tax	
		Profit	

Account Details

Account Name : _____

Name : _____

Address : _____

_____

Payment Methods

- O Cash on delivery   Amount
- O Check payment   _____
- O Direct bank transfer   Date Paid
- O PayPal   _____

Order Details

Order Number : _____

Date of order : _____

Ship date : _____

Shipping carrier : _____

Tracking ID : _____

Delivered : _____

Special option

- O Samples sent
- O Gift Message

_____

_____

Product No.	Description	Qty.	Total

Notes:

Total	
Product Cost	
Postage Cost	
Tax	
Profit	

Account Name : _____

Name : _____

Address : _____

_____

| Payment Methods |

○ Cash on delivery   Amount

○ Check payment   _____

○ Direct bank transfer   Date Paid

○ PayPal   _____

Order Number : _____

Date of order : _____

Ship date : _____

Shipping carrier : _____

Tracking ID : _____

Delivered : _____

| Special option |

○ Samples sent

○ Gift Message

_____

_____

Product No.	Description	Qty.	Total
Notes:		Total	
		Product Cost	
		Postage Cost	
		Tax	
		Profit	

Account Information

Account Name : _____

Name : _____

Address : _____

_____

Payment Methods

○ Cash on delivery   Amount

○ Check payment   _____

○ Direct bank transfer   Date Paid

○ PayPal   _____

Order Information

Order Number : _____

Date of order : _____

Ship date : _____

Shipping carrier : _____

Tracking ID : _____

Delivered : _____

Special option

○ Samples sent

○ Gift Message

_____

_____

Product No.	Description	Qty.	Total

Notes:

Total	
Product Cost	
Postage Cost	
Tax	
Profit	

Social Media Icons

Account Name : _____

Name : _____

Address : _____

_____

Payment Methods

- ○ Cash on delivery
- ○ Check payment
- ○ Direct bank transfer
- ○ PayPal

Amount

_____

Date Paid

_____

Order Number : _____

Date of order : _____

Ship date : _____

Shipping carrier : _____

Tracking ID : _____

Delivered : _____

Special option

- ○ Samples sent
- ○ Gift Message

_____

_____

Product No.	Description	Qty.	Total

Notes:

Total	
Product Cost	
Postage Cost	
Tax	
Profit	

Account Name : _____

Name : _____

Address : _____

_____

Order Number : _____

Date of order : _____

Ship date : _____

Shipping carrier : _____

Tracking ID : _____

Delivered : _____

Payment Methods

○ Cash on delivery   Amount

○ Check payment   _____

○ Direct bank transfer   Date Paid

○ PayPal   _____

Special option

○ Samples sent

○ Gift Message

_____

_____

Product No.	Description	Qty.	Total

Notes:

		Total	
		Product Cost	
		Postage Cost	
		Tax	
		Profit	

Account Info

Account Name : _____

Name : _____

Address : _____

_____

Payment Methods

- ○ Cash on delivery   Amount
- ○ Check payment   _____
- ○ Direct bank transfer   Date Paid
- ○ PayPal   _____

Order Info

Order Number : _____

Date of order : _____

Ship date : _____

Shipping carrier : _____

Tracking ID : _____

Delivered : _____

Special option

- ○ Samples sent
- ○ Gift Message

_____

_____

Product No.	Description	Qty.	Total

Notes:

	Total	
	Product Cost	
	Postage Cost	
	Tax	
	Profit	

Account Name : _____

Name : _____

Address : _____

_____

Order Number : _____

Date of order : _____

Ship date : _____

Shipping carrier : _____

Tracking ID : _____

Delivered : _____

Payment Methods

O Cash on delivery   Amount

O Check payment   _____

O Direct bank transfer   Date Paid

O PayPal   _____

Special option

O Samples sent

O Gift Message

_____

_____

Product No.	Description	Qty.	Total

Notes:

Total	
Product Cost	
Postage Cost	
Tax	
Profit	

Account Name : _____

Name : _____

Address : _____

_____

○ Cash on delivery   Amount

○ Check payment   _____

○ Direct bank transfer   Date Paid

○ PayPal   _____

Order Number : _____

Date of order : _____

Ship date : _____

Shipping carrier : _____

Tracking ID : _____

Delivered : _____

Special option

○ Samples sent

○ Gift Message

_____

_____

Product No.	Description	Qty.	Total

Notes:		Total	
		Product Cost	
		Postage Cost	
		Tax	
		Profit	

Account Information

Account Name : _____

Name : _____

Address : _____

_____

Payment Methods

- O Cash on delivery   Amount
- O Check payment   _____
- O Direct bank transfer   Date Paid
- O PayPal   _____

Order Details

Order Number : _____

Date of order : _____

Ship date : _____

Shipping carrier : _____

Tracking ID : _____

Delivered : _____

Special option

- O Samples sent
- O Gift Message

_____

_____

Product No.	Description	Qty.	Total

Notes:

Total	
Product Cost	
Postage Cost	
Tax	
Profit	

Account Name : _____

Name : _____

Address : _____

_____

○ Cash on delivery   Amount

○ Check payment   _____

○ Direct bank transfer   Date Paid

○ PayPal   _____

Order Number : _____

Date of order : _____

Ship date : _____

Shipping carrier : _____

Tracking ID : _____

Delivered : _____

Special option

○ Samples sent

○ Gift Message

_____

_____

Product No.	Description	Qty.	Total

Notes:		Total	
		Product Cost	
		Postage Cost	
		Tax	
		Profit	

Account Name : _____

Name : _____

Address : _____

_____

Order Number : _____

Date of order : _____

Ship date : _____

Shipping carrier : _____

Tracking ID : _____

Delivered : _____

Payment Methods

O Cash on delivery   Amount

O Check payment   _____

O Direct bank transfer   Date Paid

O PayPal   _____

Special option

O Samples sent

O Gift Message

_____

_____

Product No.	Description	Qty.	Total

Notes:

	Total	
	Product Cost	
	Postage Cost	
	Tax	
	Profit	

Account Name : _____

Name : _____

Address : _____

_____

Payment Methods

- O Cash on delivery   Amount
- O Check payment   _____
- O Direct bank transfer   Date Paid
- O PayPal   _____

Order Number : _____

Date of order : _____

Ship date : _____

Shipping carrier : _____

Tracking ID : _____

Delivered : _____

Special option

- O Samples sent
- O Gift Message

_____

_____

Product No.	Description	Qty.	Total

Notes:	Total	
	Product Cost	
	Postage Cost	
	Tax	
	Profit	

Account Name : _____

Name : _____

Address : _____

_____

Order Number : _____

Date of order : _____

Ship date : _____

Shipping carrier : _____

Tracking ID : _____

Delivered : _____

Payment Methods

O Cash on delivery   Amount

O Check payment   _____

O Direct bank transfer   Date Paid

O PayPal   _____

Special option

O Samples sent

O Gift Message

_____

_____

Product No.	Description	Qty.	Total

Notes:

Total	
Product Cost	
Postage Cost	
Tax	
Profit	

Social Media Icons

○ ○ ○ ○ ○ ○ ○ ○

Account Name : _____

Name : _____

Address : _____

_____

Order Number : _____

Date of order : _____

Ship date : _____

Shipping carrier : _____

Tracking ID : _____

Delivered : _____

Payment Methods

○ Cash on delivery   Amount

○ Check payment   _____

○ Direct bank transfer   Date Paid

○ PayPal   _____

Special option

○ Samples sent

○ Gift Message

_____

_____

Product No.	Description	Qty.	Total

Notes:		Total	
		Product Cost	
		Postage Cost	
		Tax	
		Profit	

Account Name : _____

Name : _____

Address : _____

_____

Payment Methods

- ○ Cash on delivery   Amount
- ○ Check payment   _____
- ○ Direct bank transfer   Date Paid
- ○ PayPal   _____

Order Number : _____

Date of order : _____

Ship date : _____

Shipping carrier : _____

Tracking ID : _____

Delivered : _____

Special option

- ○ Samples sent
- ○ Gift Message

_____

_____

Product No.	Description	Qty.	Total

Notes:

Total	
Product Cost	
Postage Cost	
Tax	
Profit	

Account Name : _____

Name : _____

Address : _____

_____

Order Number : _____

Date of order : _____

Ship date : _____

Shipping carrier : _____

Tracking ID : _____

Delivered : _____

Payment Methods

O Cash on delivery   Amount

O Check payment   _____

O Direct bank transfer   Date Paid

O PayPal   _____

Special option

O Samples sent

O Gift Message

_____

_____

Product No.	Description	Qty.	Total

Notes:		Total	
		Product Cost	
		Postage Cost	
		Tax	
		Profit	

Account Name : _____

Name : _____

Address : _____

_____

Order Number : _____

Date of order : _____

Ship date : _____

Shipping carrier : _____

Tracking ID : _____

Delivered : _____

Payment Methods

- O Cash on delivery   Amount
- O Check payment   _____
- O Direct bank transfer   Date Paid
- O PayPal   _____

Special option

- O Samples sent
- O Gift Message

_____

_____

Product No.	Description	Qty.	Total

Notes:

Total	
Product Cost	
Postage Cost	
Tax	
Profit	

Account Name : _____

Name : _____

Address : _____

_____

○ Cash on delivery   Amount

○ Check payment   _____

○ Direct bank transfer   Date Paid

○ PayPal   _____

Order Number : _____

Date of order : _____

Ship date : _____

Shipping carrier : _____

Tracking ID : _____

Delivered : _____

Special option

○ Samples sent

○ Gift Message

_____

_____

Product No.	Description	Qty.	Total

Notes:

	Total	
	Product Cost	
	Postage Cost	
	Tax	
	Profit	

Account Name : _____

Name : _____

Address : _____

_____

Payment Methods

- ○ Cash on delivery
- ○ Check payment
- ○ Direct bank transfer
- ○ PayPal

Amount

_____

Date Paid

_____

Order Number : _____

Date of order : _____

Ship date : _____

Shipping carrier : _____

Tracking ID : _____

Delivered : _____

Special option

- ○ Samples sent
- ○ Gift Message

_____

_____

Product No.	Description	Qty.	Total

Notes:

Total	
Product Cost	
Postage Cost	
Tax	
Profit	

Social Media Icons

○ ○ ○ ○ ○ ○ ○ ○

Account Name : _____

Name : _____

Address : _____

_____

Payment Methods

○ Cash on delivery   Amount

○ Check payment   _____

○ Direct bank transfer   Date Paid

○ PayPal   _____

Order Number : _____

Date of order : _____

Ship date : _____

Shipping carrier : _____

Tracking ID : _____

Delivered : _____

Special option

○ Samples sent

○ Gift Message

_____

_____

Product No.	Description	Qty.	Total

Notes:

Total	
Product Cost	
Postage Cost	
Tax	
Profit	

Account Name : _____

Name : _____

Address : _____

_____

Payment Methods

- O Cash on delivery   Amount
- O Check payment   _____
- O Direct bank transfer   Date Paid
- O PayPal   _____

Order Number : _____

Date of order : _____

Ship date : _____

Shipping carrier : _____

Tracking ID : _____

Delivered : _____

Special option

- O Samples sent
- O Gift Message

_____

_____

Product No.	Description	Qty.	Total

Notes:

Total	
Product Cost	
Postage Cost	
Tax	
Profit	

Account Name : _____

Name : _____

Address : _____

_____

Payment Methods

○ Cash on delivery   Amount

○ Check payment   _____

○ Direct bank transfer   Date Paid

○ PayPal   _____

Order Number : _____

Date of order : _____

Ship date : _____

Shipping carrier : _____

Tracking ID : _____

Delivered : _____

Special option

○ Samples sent

○ Gift Message

_____

_____

Product No.	Description	Qty.	Total

Notes:

	Total	
	Product Cost	
	Postage Cost	
	Tax	
	Profit	

Account Section

Account Name : _____

Name : _____

Address : _____

_____

Payment Methods

- ○ Cash on delivery   Amount
- ○ Check payment   _____
- ○ Direct bank transfer   Date Paid
- ○ PayPal   _____

Order Section

Order Number : _____

Date of order : _____

Ship date : _____

Shipping carrier : _____

Tracking ID : _____

Delivered : _____

Special option

- ○ Samples sent
- ○ Gift Message

_____

_____

Product No.	Description	Qty.	Total

Notes:

Total	
Product Cost	
Postage Cost	
Tax	
Profit	

Account Name : _____

Name : _____

Address : _____

_____

○ Cash on delivery   Amount

○ Check payment   _____

○ Direct bank transfer   Date Paid

○ PayPal   _____

Order Number : _____

Date of order : _____

Ship date : _____

Shipping carrier : _____

Tracking ID : _____

Delivered : _____

Special option

○ Samples sent

○ Gift Message

_____

_____

Product No.	Description	Qty.	Total
Notes:		Total	
		Product Cost	
		Postage Cost	
		Tax	
		Profit	

Account Name : _____

Name : _____

Address : _____

_____

Payment Methods

○ Cash on delivery   Amount

○ Check payment   _____

○ Direct bank transfer   Date Paid

○ PayPal   _____

Order Number : _____

Date of order : _____

Ship date : _____

Shipping carrier : _____

Tracking ID : _____

Delivered : _____

Special option

○ Samples sent

○ Gift Message

_____

_____

Product No.	Description	Qty.	Total

Notes:

Total	
Product Cost	
Postage Cost	
Tax	
Profit	

Account Name : _____

Name : _____

Address : _____

_____

Payment Methods

○ Cash on delivery   Amount

○ Check payment   _____

○ Direct bank transfer   Date Paid

○ PayPal   _____

Order Number : _____

Date of order : _____

Ship date : _____

Shipping carrier : _____

Tracking ID : _____

Delivered : _____

Special option

○ Samples sent

○ Gift Message

_____

_____

Product No.	Description	Qty.	Total

Notes:

	Total	
	Product Cost	
	Postage Cost	
	Tax	
	Profit	

○ ○ ○ ○ ○ ○ ○ ○

Account Name : _____

Name : _____

Address : _____

_____

Payment Methods

○ Cash on delivery   Amount

○ Check payment   _____

○ Direct bank transfer   Date Paid

○ PayPal   _____

Order Number : _____

Date of order : _____

Ship date : _____

Shipping carrier : _____

Tracking ID : _____

Delivered : _____

Special option

○ Samples sent

○ Gift Message

_____

_____

Product No.	Description	Qty.	Total

Notes:

Total	
Product Cost	
Postage Cost	
Tax	
Profit	

Account Name : _____

Name : _____

Address : _____

_____

○ Cash on delivery   Amount

○ Check payment   _____

○ Direct bank transfer   Date Paid

○ PayPal   _____

Order Number : _____

Date of order : _____

Ship date : _____

Shipping carrier : _____

Tracking ID : _____

Delivered : _____

Special option

○ Samples sent

○ Gift Message

_____

_____

Product No.	Description	Qty.	Total

Notes:		
	Total	
	Product Cost	
	Postage Cost	
	Tax	
	Profit	

Social Media Icons
🐦 📷 f 👻 ▶ ⓥ Ⓟ in
○ ○ ○ ○ ○ ○ ○ ○

Account Name : _____

Name : _____

Address : _____

_____

Payment Methods

○ Cash on delivery   Amount

○ Check payment   _____

○ Direct bank transfer   Date Paid

○ PayPal   _____

Order Number : _____

Date of order : _____

Ship date : _____

Shipping carrier : _____

Tracking ID : _____

Delivered : _____

Special option

○ Samples sent

○ Gift Message

_____

_____

Product No.	Description	Qty.	Total

Notes:

Total	
Product Cost	
Postage Cost	
Tax	
Profit	

Account Name : _____

Name : _____

Address : _____

_____

Order Number : _____

Date of order : _____

Ship date : _____

Shipping carrier : _____

Tracking ID : _____

Delivered : _____

Payment Methods

○ Cash on delivery   Amount

○ Check payment   _____

○ Direct bank transfer   Date Paid

○ PayPal   _____

Special option

○ Samples sent

○ Gift Message

_____

_____

Product No.	Description	Qty.	Total

Notes:	Total	
	Product Cost	
	Postage Cost	
	Tax	
	Profit	

Social media icons

(ⓣ) (ⓘ) (ⓕ) (Ⓢ) (▶) (ⓥ) (ⓟ) (ⓘⁿ)
○ ○ ○ ○ ○ ○ ○ ○

Account Name : _____

Name : _____

Address : _____

_____

Payment Methods

○ Cash on delivery   Amount

○ Check payment   _____

○ Direct bank transfer   Date Paid

○ PayPal   _____

Order Number : _____

Date of order : _____

Ship date : _____

Shipping carrier : _____

Tracking ID : _____

Delivered : _____

Special option

○ Samples sent

○ Gift Message

_____

_____

Product No.	Description	Qty.	Total

Notes:

Total	
Product Cost	
Postage Cost	
Tax	
Profit	

Account Name : _____

Name : _____

Address : _____

_____

Payment Methods

O Cash on delivery   Amount

O Check payment   _____

O Direct bank transfer   Date Paid

O PayPal   _____

Order Number : _____

Date of order : _____

Ship date : _____

Shipping carrier : _____

Tracking ID : _____

Delivered : _____

Special option

O Samples sent

O Gift Message

_____

_____

Product No.	Description	Qty.	Total

Notes:		
	Total	
	Product Cost	
	Postage Cost	
	Tax	
	Profit	

○ ○ ○ ○ ○ ○ ○ ○

Account Name : _____

Name : _____

Address : _____

_____

Order Number : _____

Date of order : _____

Ship date : _____

Shipping carrier : _____

Tracking ID : _____

Delivered : _____

Payment Methods

○ Cash on delivery   Amount

○ Check payment   _____

○ Direct bank transfer   Date Paid

○ PayPal   _____

Special option

○ Samples sent

○ Gift Message

_____

_____

Product No.	Description	Qty.	Total

Notes:

Total	
Product Cost	
Postage Cost	
Tax	
Profit	

Account Name : _____

Name : _____

Address : _____

_____

Payment Methods

○ Cash on delivery   Amount

○ Check payment   _____

○ Direct bank transfer   Date Paid

○ PayPal   _____

Order Number : _____

Date of order : _____

Ship date : _____

Shipping carrier : _____

Tracking ID : _____

Delivered : _____

Special option

○ Samples sent

○ Gift Message

_____

_____

Product No.	Description	Qty.	Total

Notes:		Total	
		Product Cost	
		Postage Cost	
		Tax	
		Profit	

Account Name : _____

Name : _____

Address : _____

_____

Order Number : _____

Date of order : _____

Ship date : _____

Shipping carrier : _____

Tracking ID : _____

Delivered : _____

Payment Methods

O Cash on delivery   Amount

O Check payment   _____

O Direct bank transfer   Date Paid

O PayPal   _____

Special option

O Samples sent

O Gift Message

_____

_____

Product No.	Description	Qty.	Total

Notes:

Total	
Product Cost	
Postage Cost	
Tax	
Profit	

Account Info

Account Name : _____

Name : _____

Address : _____

_____

Payment Methods

- ○ Cash on delivery   Amount
- ○ Check payment   _____
- ○ Direct bank transfer   Date Paid
- ○ PayPal   _____

Order Info

Order Number : _____

Date of order : _____

Ship date : _____

Shipping carrier : _____

Tracking ID : _____

Delivered : _____

Special option

- ○ Samples sent
- ○ Gift Message

_____

_____

Product No.	Description	Qty.	Total

Notes:			
	Total		
	Product Cost		
	Postage Cost		
	Tax		
	Profit		

Account Name : _____

Name : _____

Address : _____

_____

Order Number : _____

Date of order : _____

Ship date : _____

Shipping carrier : _____

Tracking ID : _____

Delivered : _____

Payment Methods

O Cash on delivery   Amount

O Check payment   _____

O Direct bank transfer   Date Paid

O PayPal   _____

Special option

O Samples sent

O Gift Message

_____

_____

Product No.	Description	Qty.	Total

Notes:

Total	
Product Cost	
Postage Cost	
Tax	
Profit	

Account Name : _____

Name : _____

Address : _____
_____

○ Cash on delivery   Amount

○ Check payment   _____

○ Direct bank transfer   Date Paid

○ PayPal   _____

Order Number : _____

Date of order : _____

Ship date : _____

Shipping carrier : _____

Tracking ID : _____

Delivered : _____

Special option

○ Samples sent

○ Gift Message

_____

_____

Product No.	Description	Qty.	Total

Notes:

Total	
Product Cost	
Postage Cost	
Tax	
Profit	

Account Name : _____

Name : _____

Address : _____

_____

Order Number : _____

Date of order : _____

Ship date : _____

Shipping carrier : _____

Tracking ID : _____

Delivered : _____

Payment Methods

- O Cash on delivery
- O Check payment
- O Direct bank transfer
- O PayPal

Amount

_____

Date Paid

_____

Special option

- O Samples sent
- O Gift Message

_____

_____

Product No.	Description	Qty.	Total

Notes:

Total	
Product Cost	
Postage Cost	
Tax	
Profit	

Account

Account Name : _____

Name : _____

Address : _____

_____

Payment Methods

O Cash on delivery   Amount

O Check payment   _____

O Direct bank transfer   Date Paid

O PayPal   _____

Order Number : _____

Date of order : _____

Ship date : _____

Shipping carrier : _____

Tracking ID : _____

Delivered : _____

Special option

O Samples sent

O Gift Message

_____

_____

Product No.	Description	Qty.	Total

Notes:

Total	
Product Cost	
Postage Cost	
Tax	
Profit	

Social Media Icons

Account Name : _____

Name : _____

Address : _____

_____

Payment Methods

O Cash on delivery   Amount

O Check payment   _____

O Direct bank transfer   Date Paid

O PayPal   _____

Order Number : _____

Date of order : _____

Ship date : _____

Shipping carrier : _____

Tracking ID : _____

Delivered : _____

Special option

O Samples sent

O Gift Message

_____

_____

Product No.	Description	Qty.	Total

Notes:

Total	
Product Cost	
Postage Cost	
Tax	
Profit	

Account Name : _____

Name : _____

Address : _____

_____

Payment Methods

○ Cash on delivery   Amount

○ Check payment   _____

○ Direct bank transfer   Date Paid

○ PayPal   _____

Order Number : _____

Date of order : _____

Ship date : _____

Shipping carrier : _____

Tracking ID : _____

Delivered : _____

Special option

○ Samples sent

○ Gift Message

_____

_____

Product No.	Description	Qty.	Total
Notes:		Total	
		Product Cost	
		Postage Cost	
		Tax	
		Profit	

Account Name : _____

Name : _____

Address : _____

_____

Order Number : _____

Date of order : _____

Ship date : _____

Shipping carrier : _____

Tracking ID : _____

Delivered : _____

Payment Methods

- ⭘ Cash on delivery   Amount
- ⭘ Check payment   _____
- ⭘ Direct bank transfer   Date Paid
- ⭘ PayPal   _____

Special option

- ⭘ Samples sent
- ⭘ Gift Message

_____

_____

Product No.	Description	Qty.	Total

Notes:

Total	
Product Cost	
Postage Cost	
Tax	
Profit	

Account Name : _____

Name : _____

Address : _____

_____

Payment Methods

- ○ Cash on delivery   Amount
- ○ Check payment   _____
- ○ Direct bank transfer   Date Paid
- ○ PayPal   _____

Order Number : _____

Date of order : _____

Ship date : _____

Shipping carrier : _____

Tracking ID : _____

Delivered : _____

Special option

- ○ Samples sent
- ○ Gift Message

_____

_____

Product No.	Description	Qty.	Total

Notes:		
	Total	
	Product Cost	
	Postage Cost	
	Tax	
	Profit	

Account Information

Account Name : _____

Name : _____

Address : _____

_____

Payment Methods

- O Cash on delivery   Amount
- O Check payment   _____
- O Direct bank transfer   Date Paid
- O PayPal   _____

Order Information

Order Number : _____

Date of order : _____

Ship date : _____

Shipping carrier : _____

Tracking ID : _____

Delivered : _____

Special option

- O Samples sent
- O Gift Message

_____

_____

Product No.	Description	Qty.	Total

Notes:

Total	
Product Cost	
Postage Cost	
Tax	
Profit	

Account Name : _____

Name : _____

Address : _____

_____

Payment Methods

○ Cash on delivery   Amount

○ Check payment   _____

○ Direct bank transfer   Date Paid

○ PayPal   _____

Order Number : _____

Date of order : _____

Ship date : _____

Shipping carrier : _____

Tracking ID : _____

Delivered : _____

Special option

○ Samples sent

○ Gift Message

_____

_____

Product No.	Description	Qty.	Total

Notes:

	Total	
	Product Cost	
	Postage Cost	
	Tax	
	Profit	

Account Name : _____

Name : _____

Address : _____

_____

Order Number : _____

Date of order : _____

Ship date : _____

Shipping carrier : _____

Tracking ID : _____

Delivered : _____

Payment Methods

○ Cash on delivery   Amount

○ Check payment   _____

○ Direct bank transfer   Date Paid

○ PayPal   _____

Special option

○ Samples sent

○ Gift Message

_____

_____

Product No.	Description	Qty.	Total

Notes:

Total	
Product Cost	
Postage Cost	
Tax	
Profit	

Account details

Account Name : _____

Name : _____

Address : _____

_____

Payment Methods

- ○ Cash on delivery
- ○ Check payment
- ○ Direct bank transfer
- ○ PayPal

Amount

_____

Date Paid

_____

Order Number : _____

Date of order : _____

Ship date : _____

Shipping carrier : _____

Tracking ID : _____

Delivered : _____

Special option

- ○ Samples sent
- ○ Gift Message

_____

_____

Product No.	Description	Qty.	Total

Notes:			
	Total		
	Product Cost		
	Postage Cost		
	Tax		
	Profit		

Account Name : _____

Name : _____

Address : _____

_____

Payment Methods

○ Cash on delivery   Amount

○ Check payment   _____

○ Direct bank transfer   Date Paid

○ PayPal   _____

Order Number : _____

Date of order : _____

Ship date : _____

Shipping carrier : _____

Tracking ID : _____

Delivered : _____

Special option

○ Samples sent

○ Gift Message

_____

_____

Product No.	Description	Qty.	Total

Notes:

Total	
Product Cost	
Postage Cost	
Tax	
Profit	

Social Media Icons

○ ○ ○ ○ ○ ○ ○ ○

Account Name : _____

Name : _____

Address : _____

_____

Payment Methods

○ Cash on delivery   Amount

○ Check payment   _____

○ Direct bank transfer   Date Paid

○ PayPal   _____

Order Number : _____

Date of order : _____

Ship date : _____

Shipping carrier : _____

Tracking ID : _____

Delivered : _____

Special option

○ Samples sent

○ Gift Message

_____

_____

Product No.	Description	Qty.	Total

Notes:

Total	
Product Cost	
Postage Cost	
Tax	
Profit	

Social Media Icons

Account Name : _____

Name : _____

Address : _____

_____

Payment Methods

- ○ Cash on delivery **Amount**
- ○ Check payment _____
- ○ Direct bank transfer **Date Paid**
- ○ PayPal _____

Order Number : _____

Date of order : _____

Ship date : _____

Shipping carrier : _____

Tracking ID : _____

Delivered : _____

Special option

- ○ Samples sent
- ○ Gift Message

_____

_____

Product No.	Description	Qty.	Total

Notes:

Total	
Product Cost	
Postage Cost	
Tax	
Profit	

Notes

Notes

Printed in Great Britain
by Amazon